THE REAL DEAL

HOW MONEY AND MARKETS ACTUALLY WORKS

SAGE THOMPSON

Copyright © 2024 by Sage Thompson

All rights reserved.

No part of this publication may be reproduced, distributed, or transmitted in any form or by any means, including photocopying, recording, or other electronic or mechanical methods, without the prior written permission of the publisher, except in the case of brief quotations embodied in critical reviews and certain other noncommercial uses permitted by copyright law.

The information in this book is true and complete to the best of our knowledge. All recommendations are made without guarantee on the part of the author or publisher. The author and publisher disclaim any liability in connection with the use of information

Table of contents

INTRODUCTION 5
    Why Understanding Money and Markets Matters 5
    The Journey Ahead: What to Expect 9

CHAPTER 1 15
THE BASIS OF MONEY 15
    The Evolution of Money 15
    What's the Point of Money? 18
    The Role of Banks 22
    Central Banking 25

CHAPTER 2 31
MARKETS AND THEIR MECHANICS 31
    Investments 31
    The Financial Industry 35
    How to Trade Forex 38
    The Commodities Market 41

CHAPTER 3 47
CONCEPTS AND METHODS 47
    Demand and Supply 47
    Market Structures 50
    Behavioral Economics 53
    Financial Instruments 56

CHAPTER 4 61
THE PARTICIPANTS AND THE FIELD OF PLAY 61
    Institutional Investors 61
    Retail Investors 65
    Policies and Regulators 68

CHAPTER 5	**75**
WORLDWIDE VIEWS	**75**
International Trade	75
Emerging Markets	79
Economic Indicators	82
CHAPTER 6	**87**
REAL-WORLD APPLICATIONS	**87**
Personal Finance	87
Financial Management	91
Financial Disasters	94
CHAPTER 7	**101**
THE FUTURE OF MONEY AND MARKETS	**101**
Innovation and Fintech	101
Sustainable Investing	105
Forecasting Trends in the Market	109
CONCLUSION	**115**
Integrating Information	115
Keeping Up-to-Date	117

INTRODUCTION

Welcome to "The Real Deal: The True Story of Money and Markets. Whether you're an experienced investor, an economics student, or just interested in the financial world, this book aims to explain the complexity of money and markets in an approachable and understandable manner. We're going to go on an adventure that reveals the complex workings of the financial institutions that influence our daily existence.

Why Understanding Money and Markets Matters

The Basis of Contemporary Society

Money is our economy's lifeblood and more than simply money. It powers companies, covers expenses for services, and aids in our own accomplishments. Have you ever thought, however, what makes money valuable? Why do we put our faith in printed documents or digital account numbers? The development and operation of money, which we will examine in this book, hold the keys to the solutions.

Since markets and money are the cornerstones of contemporary civilization, understanding them is essential. These basic ideas affect every transaction, from purchasing groceries to making stock investments. A thorough understanding of money and markets enables people to make wise financial choices, which promotes both economic and personal development.

Individual Self-Empowerment

The importance of financial literacy has increased in the fast-paced world of today. Many individuals leave their financial choices to chance or to people who may not have their best interests at heart because they feel overwhelmed by financial jargon and market swings. By arming you with the information to take charge of your financial future, this book seeks to alter that.

Being financially literate gives you the ability to make wise financial decisions, save for the future, and steer clear of frequent traps. It makes it possible for you to comprehend investment possibilities, negotiate complicated financial instruments, and identify economic trends that may have an influence on your life. With this information, you may make wise decisions that support your objectives and moral principles and attain financial security and stability.

Financial Intelligence

Understanding markets and money on a larger scale is crucial to understanding how the world economy functions. Because economies are interrelated, developments in one region of the globe may have a significant impact on another. For example, a collapse in the US stock market may affect economies all across the globe, affecting currency rates, employment markets, and even political stability.

Gaining knowledge about money and markets may help you grasp the larger economic dynamics at work. Being aware of these things keeps you up-to-date on world events and how they could affect your financial situation. It also makes it possible for you to contribute to a more educated and involved society by improving your ability to participate in conversations on economic issues.

The Journey Ahead: What to Expect

A Methodical Approach

This book is divided into many sections, each of which builds upon the one before it to provide the reader with a thorough grasp of money and markets. We'll begin by going over the fundamentals, like the origins and development of money, before moving on to trickier ideas like financial instruments, market dynamics, and worldwide economic patterns.

The Money Foundations

We start our adventure from the beginning and follow the development of money, from ancient barter systems to modern digital currencies. You will discover the qualities that characterize money, its many manifestations, and the crucial function that banks and central banks play in our financial system. You will get a firm understanding of what money is and how it works in the economy by reading this section.

Markets and How They Work
We'll explore the realm of markets next. You will learn about the workings of several markets, including commodities, foreign currency, and stock and bond markets. We'll demystify the intricate workings of these marketplaces, including the factors that affect market behavior and how prices are set. You will acquire the information in this part to comprehend market dynamics and make wise investing choices.

Concepts and Methods
We'll look at important economic theories and methods that support market behavior in this section. Behavioral economics, market

structures, and supply and demand will all be covered. We'll also discuss the goals and dangers of financial products like futures, options, and derivatives. You'll get a stronger comprehension of the guiding principles of economic and financial decision-making by reading this section.

The Participants and the Field of Play

It is essential to comprehend the major actors in the financial markets. You will learn about regulators, ordinary investors, and institutional investors in this section. You'll discover the functions they fulfill, the tactics they use, and the effects they have on the markets. You'll have a better understanding of the financial scene and the many forces involved with this information.

Worldwide Views

Markets and money are worldwide phenomena that are not limited to any one nation. We'll look at economic indicators, developing markets, and international commerce in this section. You'll learn about the workings of international markets, the potential and hazards of developing economies, and the importance of economic metrics like GDP, inflation, and employment rates. You will learn more about the global backdrop of money and markets by reading this section.

Practical Uses

While theory is vital, it all comes together in real practice. We'll talk about corporate finance, personal money, and economic crises in this part. You'll discover how to put the principles you've studied into practice by managing your own money, comprehending business financial plans, and identifying the origins and effects of financial crises. You will feel more confident navigating the financial world with this information.

The Markets and Money of the Future

The world of finance is ever-changing. The future of money and markets will be examined in this last segment, where we'll look at topics including fintech innovation, digital currencies, and sustainable investment. You will gain knowledge of the most recent advancements and how they could affect the financial scene. You can stay on top of trends and be ready for the future by reading this section.

Resources and Conclusion

We'll summarize the information you've learned and provide helpful advice for furthering your financial education at the end. In order to assist you in continuing your education, we'll also offer appendices with a dictionary of important words, suggested readings, and helpful links and resources.

You will have a thorough knowledge of how money and markets function by the conclusion of this book. You'll possess the information necessary to comprehend economic events, make wise financial choices, and confidently negotiate the complexity of the financial world. Together, let's go out on this adventure to learn the truth about markets and money.

CHAPTER 1

THE BASIS OF MONEY

The Evolution of Money

Barter to Bitcoin Transition

Fundamentally, money is a convenience mechanism that makes it possible for people to exchange commodities and services effectively. Prior to the invention of money, communities depended on barter systems, in which individuals would directly swap one commodity or service for another. This method had serious drawbacks, even if it functioned well in tiny, tight-knit groups. In order to barter, two people had to have what the other desired and value it equally, which meant that there had to be a double coincidence of desires.

Barter's shortcomings resulted in the creation of commodity money—items having inherent worth that are used as a means of trade. Cattle, cereals, and precious metals are a few examples. Metals gained widespread acceptance because of their mobility, durability, and divisibility—gold and silver in particular.

The invention of coinage marked the next major advance. To guarantee constant value and ease commerce over wider areas, governments started to produce uniform coins. Because coins made it simpler to calculate prices and accumulate money, their usage signaled a significant step towards the development of a more complex economic system.

The drawbacks of carrying a lot of coinage became apparent as trade routes expanded and sophisticated civilizations developed. The creation of paper money resulted from this.

Paper money was first used in China in the Tang Dynasty as a guarantee from the issuer to pay the bearer a certain sum in coins or goods. The idea revolutionized international trade and made its way to Europe and the Middle East.

Another significant advancement occurred in the 20th century with the advent of fiat money, which is money that has value based on government edicts rather than actual goods. Fiat money depends on both economic stability and public confidence in the body that issues it. The emergence of electronic payments and digital currency around this time also revolutionized the way that transactions were carried out.

As a new kind of digital currency and a means of decentralizing money, cryptocurrencies like Bitcoin are gaining popularity today. Blockchain technology, a safe, open ledger system that keeps track of every transaction, was first presented with Bitcoin, a cryptocurrency founded in 2009 by an unknown person going by the name Satoshi Nakamoto. Cryptocurrencies provide an alternative to established financial institutions for the storage and transfer of wealth.

The development of money, from the antiquated barter systems to the advanced realm of digital currencies, is a reflection of humankind's search for more dependable and effective means of exchange and value storage. Every phase of this development has created more sophisticated and adaptable financial systems by building on the knowledge gained in earlier times.

What's the Point of Money?

Characteristics and Definitions

Money is often characterized by its features and purposes that set it apart from other assets. Fundamentally, money is used as a store of value, a unit of account, a means of trade, and sometimes as a standard for postponed payment.

Medium of Exchange: By removing the need for a double coincidence of desires, money makes transactions easier. In commerce, it serves as a middleman and is accepted by all parties in return for products and services.

Unit of Account: Comparing prices and keeping track of debts is made simpler by the standard measure that money offers for the valuation of commodities and services. Accounting and economic computations are made easier by this feature.

Store of worth: Cash maintains its worth over time and may be stored for later use. This quality enables people to postpone spending and budget for future costs.

Standard of Deferred Payment: Payment for obligations that are due later is commonly accepted. Credit and lending systems are supported by this function.

Money has to have certain qualities in order to successfully carry out these functions:

Durability: Over time, money must be able to survive physical deterioration. Durable money includes metals like gold and silver as well as contemporary polymer currencies.

Portability: People should be able to carry money readily for transactions if it is easily transportable. Digital currencies, paper money, and coins are all quite portable.

Divisibility: To facilitate transactions of various sizes, money needs to be divided into smaller denominations. Money may be utilized for both big and minor transactions thanks to this feature.

Uniformity: The value of every coin should be the same as that of other coins of the same denomination. Consistency and equity in transactions are guaranteed by standardization.

Limited quantity: In order to preserve its value, money must have a limited quantity. Money that is produced or issued in excess may cause inflation and value loss.

Acceptability: The use of money as a means of trade has to be generally accepted. Its value stems from the community's mutual trust and appreciation of its value.

We may better appreciate what makes money dependable and efficient by knowing these definitions and traits. The transition from tangible goods to virtual currency serves as an example of how we are always innovating and adapting in our pursuit of the ideal medium of exchange.

The Role of Banks

From Loans to Savings

Because banks act as middlemen between savers and borrowers, they are essential to the operation of contemporary economies. Their function goes beyond only preserving cash; they also aid in the growth and stability of the economy.

Taking Deposits: Taking deposits from both people and companies is one of the main duties of banks. These deposits may be made into fixed deposits, checking, or savings accounts. Through the consolidation of cash from several depositors, banks establish a significant capital reserve.

Offering Loans: Banks lend money to people, companies, and governments using the money that is deposited. These loans may be used for a number of things, such as building infrastructure, expanding businesses, or financing personal expenses. Banks promote development and economic activity by making loans.

Supporting Payments: Banks provide debit cards, checks, and electronic transfers, among other necessary payment services. These services make it possible for parties to trade with ease, which improves economic efficiency.

Investment Services: Banks also provide investment services, assisting clients in building their wealth via stocks, bonds, mutual funds, and other financial instruments. These services meet their customers' various risk tolerances and financial demands.

Risk Management: Using sophisticated risk assessment procedures and diversification, banks are essential in controlling financial risks. Banks reduce the effect of prospective losses by distributing their assets across different industries and geographical areas.

Currency Exchange: Banks provide their clients access to foreign currencies by facilitating currency exchange for commerce and travel abroad. This service facilitates cross-border financial transactions and international trade.

Financial advising: Banks often give firms and people advising services, supplying knowledge and tactics for efficient money management. Investment plans, tax optimization, and retirement planning are a few examples of this advice.

Beyond facilitating specific transactions, banks also have an impact on the whole economy. Banks contribute to the stability and expansion of the economy by controlling the flow of credit and money. Their capacity to evaluate and control risk guarantees the effective distribution of resources, promoting a strong and stable financial system.

Central Banking

Monetary policy and the Federal Reserve

In contemporary economies, central banks play a crucial role as regulators of the monetary system and guarantees of financial stability. The Federal Reserve, sometimes known as the Fed, is the central bank of the United States.

Regulating Money Supply: Controlling the money supply is one of central banks' main responsibilities. The discount rate, reserve requirements, and open market operations are only a few of the instruments the Federal Reserve utilizes to control the quantity of money in circulation.

Open Market Operations: To manage the money supply, this entails purchasing and disposing of government securities. The money supply is increased in the economy when the Fed purchases securities. On the other hand, selling securities takes money out of circulation and lowers the money supply.

Reserve Requirements: The minimum quantity of reserves that banks are required to keep against deposits is determined by central banks. The quantity of money banks are able to lend may be changed by the Fed by changing these restrictions.

Discount Rate: The interest rate at which commercial banks may borrow money from the central bank is known as the discount rate.

Raising the discount rate has the opposite impact of lowering it, which promotes borrowing and expands the money supply.

Monetary Policy: To accomplish certain economic objectives, such as regulating employment levels, preventing inflation, and maintaining reasonable long-term interest rates, the Federal Reserve develops and carries out monetary policy.

Inflation Control: The Fed attempts to maintain inflation within a target range by modifying the money supply and interest rates. Maintaining the consistent buying power of money is ensured by controlling inflation.

Employment Management: By implementing monetary policy, the Fed seeks to maximize employment. Reduced interest rates encourage borrowing and investment, which boosts the economy and creates jobs.

Stability of Interest Rates: Predictability in the economy fosters investment and consumption, and stable long-term interest rates contribute to this.

Lender of Last Resort: In times of financial hardship, central banks serve as the banking system's lender of last resort. The Fed contributes to preserving financial stability and averting banking panics by providing emergency financing to banks that are experiencing a lack of liquidity.

Supervision and Regulation: To guarantee banks' soundness and adherence to legal requirements, the Federal Reserve supervises and controls them. This oversight contributes to consumer protection and maintains the financial system's credibility.

Financial Services: In addition to issuing money and overseeing the country's payment networks, central banks also provide other financial services. The seamless operation of the financial infrastructure is guaranteed by these services.

The economy is greatly impacted by the central bank's decisions. The goal of the Federal Reserve's policy making and regulation is to provide a sound and stable economic environment. We can better grasp the workings of our financial system and the strategies used to overcome obstacles in the economy by knowing the roles and responsibilities of central banks.

We have looked at the basics of money in this first section of *The Real Deal: How Money and Markets Actually Work. We have paved the way for a greater comprehension of the financial systems that influence our world, from their genesis and basic features to the vital roles

performed by banks and central banks. As we
As we go along, we'll expand on this

understanding to learn more about the complex mechanisms behind markets and the economic theories that underpin them.

CHAPTER 2

MARKETS AND THEIR MECHANICS

Investments

The Trading and Valuation of Stocks

Investors purchase and sell ownership holdings in public corporations in the dynamic stock market. We refer to these ownership positions as shares or stocks. The stock market is vital to the economy because it gives businesses the funding they need to expand and gives investors a chance to benefit from their successes.

How to Trade Stocks

Exchanges such as the Nasdaq and the New York Stock Exchange (NYSE) are used for stock trading. These online marketplaces make it easier to purchase and sell equities while maintaining efficiency and transparency. The two basic categories of trading are primary and secondary.

Primary Market: An initial public offering (IPO) is how a corporation issues new shares when it goes public for the first time. These shares are purchased by investors straight from the business, giving it the funding it needs.

Secondary Market: Shares are exchanged among investors on the secondary market after the IPO. Existing shares are exchanged here without the issuing firm being directly involved.

Various orders may be used to perform trades:

Market Orders: Purchase or sell orders that are carried out right away at the going rate.

Limit Orders: Purchase or sell orders that can only be carried out at a certain price or above.

Stop Orders: Orders that, when a certain price is achieved, turn into market orders.

How Equities Are Calculated

Making wise financial choices requires a thorough understanding of stock valuation. Technical analysis and fundamental analysis are the two main approaches.

Fundamental Analysis: This approach assesses the fundamental worth of a business by looking at its profits, sales, growth prospects, and debt loads. To ascertain a stock's fair value, analysts consider industry circumstances, quality of management, and financial statements.

Technical Analysis: This approach is based on past trade volumes and price movements. Technical analysts forecast future price movements based on historical market behavior using charts and indicators.

Important indicators for stock value include:

Price-to-Earnings (P/E) Ratio: The current share price of a business divided by its earnings per share. An overpriced stock may be indicated by a high P/E ratio, while an undervalued company may be suggested by a low P/E ratio.

Dividend Yield: The percentage representation of the yearly dividend payment divided by the stock price. For investors looking for income, this indicator is essential.

Book Value: The difference between an entity's net worth of assets and liabilities. A stock's overvaluation or undervaluation may be determined by comparing its price to its book value.

Investors may balance risks and rewards in their portfolios by making strategic choices based on their understanding of how equities are priced and traded.

The Financial Industry

Interest Rates and Debt Instruments

Investors purchase and sell debt instruments on the expansive bond market. In essence, bonds are loans from investors to borrowers, usually governments or businesses, with the principal returned at maturity and periodic interest payments.

Bond Types

Government Bonds: These are low-risk investments that are issued by national governments. U.S. One such example is Treasury bonds.

Municipal Bonds: Usually offering tax-exempt interest income, these bonds are issued by state and municipal governments.

Corporate Bonds: Generally offering greater rates than government bonds, these bonds are issued by firms to raise cash.

The Function of Bonds

Purchasing a bond entails making a fixed-term loan to the issuer. The issuer agrees to repay the principal amount at the bond's maturity and to pay you monthly interest in the form of coupon payments.

Bond Prices and Interest Rates

In the bond market, interest rates are quite important. Bond prices decrease as interest rates rise, and vice versa. Because new bonds are issued at current interest rates, old bonds with lower rates become less appealing, leading to an inverse relationship.

Metrics of Yield

Bond yields are evaluated by investors using a number of metrics, including:

Current Yield: The bond's current price divided by the yearly coupon payment.

Yield to Maturity (YTM): The total expected return on a bond, after deducting the face value from the purchase price and all coupon payments, if held until it matures.

Yield Spread: The variation in yields across bond classes, sometimes used to contrast the risk profiles of different issuers.

Comprehending the bond market necessitates having a solid understanding of debt instruments, interest rate dynamics, and yield evaluation metrics. With fixed-income investments, this information aids investors in risk management and helps them reach their financial objectives.

How to Trade Forex

A Guide to Currency Trading

The world's biggest and most liquid financial market is the foreign exchange, or FX, market, where currencies are exchanged continuously. Due to its ability to convert one currency into another, the forex market is crucial for both people and corporations engaged in international commerce and investment.

The Operation of the Forex Market

Trading currencies entails purchasing one currency and selling another at the same time. Currency pairings, such as EUR/USD (euro/US dollar) or GBP/JPY (British pound/Japanese yen), are used in forex trading. The base currency is the first one in the pair, while the quote currency is the second.

Notable Attendees

Commercial Banks: Perform speculative trading and assist customers with currency exchange.

Central Banks: Through monetary policy and actions, they affect the value of currencies.

Corporations: Manage corporate operations in several currencies by engaging in currency transactions.

Retail traders are profit-seeking individual investors who often use internet platforms.

A Factor Affecting Exchange Rates

Interest Rates: As a result of drawing in foreign money, higher interest rates cause currency values to rise.

Economic Indicators: Information on inflation, employment rates, and GDP growth affects the value of currencies.

Political Stability: The currencies of nations with stable political systems tend to be stronger.

Market Sentiment: Short-term currency fluctuations may be influenced by traders' opinions and expectations.

Strategies for Trading

Scalping: Consists of several little deals to profit from slight price fluctuations.

Day Trading: Concentrates on brief changes in price throughout a single trading day.

Swing Trading: Looks to capitalize on changes in price that occur over a few days or weeks.

Position trading: Positions are held for longer periods of time, depending on long-term market patterns.

Due to its volatility and complexity, the currency market presents both possibilities and threats. An investor may successfully navigate this volatile market by having a solid grasp of how currency trading operates and the variables that impact exchange rates.

The Commodities Market

Trading Resources: Gold, Oil, and Other

Raw resources and primary goods, including gold, oil, agricultural products, and metals, are traded on the commodities market. Trading in commodities is vital to the global economy because it provides consumers and companies with resources.

Commercial Types

Precious Metals: Palladium, platinum, silver,

and gold are among them. These metals are prized for their industrial uses and scarcity.

Electricity Commodities: Consists of coal, natural gas, and crude oil. Commodities for energy are essential for sustaining economies.

Agricultural Commodities: Contains animals like pigs and cattle as well as crops like wheat, corn, and soybeans. These goods are necessary for the manufacturing of food.

Industrial Metals: These include zinc, aluminum, and copper, which are essential for building and industry.

How to Trade Commodities

Exchanges such as the Chicago Mercantile Exchange (CME) and the New York Mercantile Exchange (NYMEX) are venues for trading commodities. Futures contracts or spot contracts may be used for trading.

Spot Contracts: These include the acquisition and delivery of goods right away.

Futures Contracts: Deals to purchase or sell a good at a fixed price at a later time. Producers and consumers may protect themselves against price volatility by using futures contracts.

Commodity Price Influencing Factors

Supply and Demand: The fundamental concepts of supply and demand have a big influence on commodity pricing. A commodity's price might increase or decrease based on its scarcity or availability.

Geopolitical Events: Trade policy, political unrest, and supply chain disruptions may all have an impact on pricing.

Weather Conditions: Crop yields may be

impacted by weather patterns, which are especially sensitive to agricultural commodities.

Economic Data: Demand for different commodities is influenced by indicators like industrial output and inventory levels.

Strategies for Trading

Hedging: This refers to utilizing futures contracts as a hedge against changes in price. Hedging is a common way for producers and consumers to control costs.

Speculation: Traders engage in greater risk/reward trading by purchasing and selling commodities in an attempt to benefit from price fluctuations.

Arbitrage: This is the practice of profitably using pricing discrepancies across marketplaces while assuming the least amount of risk.

It is necessary to understand the many kinds of commodities, how they are exchanged, and the variables affecting their pricing in order to comprehend the commodities market. With this information, investors may control the risks associated with resource-dependent companies and diversify their portfolios.

We have learned about the workings of different financial markets in this second installment of "The Real Deal: How Money and Markets Actually Work. Every market in the world economy, from the humming stock exchanges to the complex bond market, the enormous FX market, and the vital commodities market, is vital to the other markets. Investors may traverse the financial environment with confidence and make well-informed judgments if they have a solid grasp of these markets' dynamics.

47

CHAPTER 3

CONCEPTS AND METHODS

Demand and Supply

The Market-Driving Forces

The basic factors that drive markets, shape prices, and decide how resources are allocated are supply and demand. Gaining an understanding of these influences is essential to understanding how markets work and how prices are set.

Demand Law

According to the law of demand, the quantity desired rises as an item or service's price drops, and vice versa, all other things being equal. Consumer behavior is the driving force behind this inverse relationship: items with lower pricing are more appealing to consumers.

Supply Law

On the other hand, the law of supply states that as an item or service's price rises, its supply also rises, and vice versa, all other things being equal. Producers are encouraged to provide more when prices are higher because they can make more money.

State of Balance

The market equilibrium is reached when the amounts provided and requested are equal. This is determined by the interplay of supply and demand. The market price now stabilizes and is not under any intrinsic pressure to move.

Modifications in Supply and Demand

Because the market is dynamic, a number of things may cause the supply and demand curves to shift:

Demand Shifters: The demand curve may be shifted by variations in income, tastes and preferences, the cost of associated commodities, buyer expectations, and the quantity of purchases.

Supply Shifters: The supply curve may be shifted by changes to manufacturing technology, input costs, seller numbers, and expectations.

Stiffness

The degree to which the amount provided or required adapts to price fluctuations is known as elasticity. When a price changes little, the supply or demand of items with high price elasticity varies significantly, while inelastic commodities see little change in either way.

You can study market trends and forecast how changes in different aspects will affect pricing and quantities by having a solid understanding of supply and demand.

Market Structures

Ideal Rivalry to Monopoly

Market structures provide an explanation of the competitive landscape that businesses compete in. These market systems, which vary from monopolies to perfect competition, each have unique traits and effects on consumer behavior.

Fine Competition

A market with perfect competition is one in which several small businesses offer the same goods. Everyone participating has complete knowledge, and there are no obstacles to entering or leaving. In the long term, this system allocates resources efficiently and yields modest profits since aberrant earnings draw in new players until equilibrium is restored.

Competitive Monopoly

In monopolistic competition, several businesses provide unique items. Because of product differentiation, each company has some market strength, but competition is still fierce. Competition among businesses in terms of pricing, quality, and marketing results in a wide range of goods and inventions. Clothing labels and the restaurant business are two examples.

Oligopoly

A few powerful companies control a large portion of the market in an oligopoly. These companies have a lot of market power, and what they do may have a big effect on the state of the market. Interdependence is a defining feature of oligopolistic marketplaces, where businesses must take competitors' possible responses to adjustments in pricing or production into account. The car and aviation sectors are two examples.

Monopoly

When one company dominates the whole market for a product or service and there are no viable alternatives, it is said to have a monopoly. High entry barriers hinder other businesses from joining the market. Price and production thresholds may be established by monopolists to optimize profits. However, since there is less competition, monopolies may result in inefficiency and damage to consumers. Utility businesses often function as monopolies under regulation.

Gaining insight into the intricacies of economic relationships is possible by comprehending market structures, which aid in explaining corporate behavior and the consequences of the market.

Behavioral Economics

Emotions in Investing Decisions

Behavioral economics combines economic theory and psychological insights to study how individuals make financial choices. While behavioral economics recognizes that people often behave irrationally, traditional economics makes the assumption that people make logical decisions.

Memory Biases

Financial choices are influenced by many cognitive biases.

Anchoring: Making judgments by placing an excessive amount of weight on the first fact that is learned (the "anchor"). For example, in discussions, the final negotiated price may differ from the original price offered.

Loss Aversion: The propensity to value averting losses above reaping comparable benefits. Investing behavior that is risk-averse may result from this bias.

Overconfidence: The tendency to overestimate one's expertise or aptitude, which may result in excessively hazardous investments or an underestimate of possible losses.

Herd Behavior: following others' lead instead of exercising independent judgment, which often results in bubble bursts and market collapses.

Asset Theory

Prospect theory, which was developed by Amos Tversky and Daniel Kahneman, explains how humans make decisions about probabilistic choices that include risk. It demonstrates how people's values for profits and losses vary, which causes them to make irrational judgments. People, for instance, are more likely to take on risks in order to prevent losses than to avoid risks when contemplating possible rewards.

Incentives

Nudges are small adjustments made to the decision architecture or environment to affect behavior without limiting possibilities. When workers are automatically enrolled in retirement savings programs, for example, participation rates are higher than when they must voluntarily join.

People and politicians may create more effective financial plans and interventions that take into consideration the complexity and irrationality of human behavior by having a better knowledge of behavioral economics.

Financial Instruments

Futures, Options, and Derivatives

Contracts, known as financial instruments, provide one party with a financial asset and another party with a financial obligation. In today's financial markets, sophisticated products like futures, options, and derivatives are essential.

Alternatives

The value of a derivative comes from an underlying asset, which might be currencies, equities, bonds, or commodities. Typical derivative forms consist of:

Swaps are agreements between parties to swap cash flows or other financial instruments. Two common examples are interest rate swaps and currency swaps.

Futures: contracts to purchase or sell an item at a fixed price at a certain future date. Exchanges handle the standardization and trading of futures.

Forwards: customized contracts sold over-the-counter (OTC) that resemble futures.

Choices

Options provide the holder with the right, but not the duty, to purchase or sell an asset within a certain time frame at a given price. There are mostly two kinds:

Call Options: Assign the holder the right, prior to the option's expiration, to purchase an asset at a predetermined price (the striking price).

Put Options: These allow the holder to sell an item before the option expires at a predetermined price.

Options are written (sold contracts of options) and utilized for revenue generation, speculating, and hedging.

Futures

Contracts for futures require the seller to sell an item at a particular price on a given future date and the buyer to acquire it at that price. Futures are used for both price movement speculation and hedging against variations in price. Futures lower counterparty risk since they are standardized and traded on exchanges, in contrast to forwards.

Speculation and Hedging

Hedging: using derivatives to balance possible losses from other assets in order to lower risk. A farmer may, for instance, utilize futures contracts to fix crop prices and guard against drops in those prices.

Speculation: Making money off of predicted price changes by using derivatives. Speculation is risky, even if it has the potential to be very profitable.

Investors may control risk, leverage their assets, and increase portfolio returns by having a solid understanding of financial products, including derivatives, options, and futures. Although these tools provide flexibility and potential, they also call for skill and careful thought.

We've covered both the theoretical and applied parts of economics and finance in this third section of *The Real Deal: How Money and Markets Actually Work. Every subject that we cover deepens our grasp of the workings of markets, from the basic laws of supply and demand to the intricate workings of market structures, psychological factors influencing financial choices, and the nuances of financial instruments. Equipped with this understanding, you may more skillfully traverse the financial landscape and make well-informed choices that suit your objectives and risk tolerance.

CHAPTER 4

THE PARTICIPANTS AND THE FIELD OF PLAY

Institutional Investors

Mutual funds, pension funds, and hedge funds

The titans of the financial markets, institutional investors, oversee enormous quantities of capital on behalf of their customers. These consist of pension funds, mutual funds, and hedge funds, each of which has a unique function within the market ecology.

Funds for Hedge Funds

Private investment vehicles known as hedge funds use a variety of tactics to produce large returns, sometimes at significant risk. They are renowned for their ability to make a variety of investment decisions, such as trading in derivatives, short sales, and leverage. Institutional investors and high-net-worth individuals are the usual clients of hedge funds.

Strategies: A variety of strategies, including long/short equities, market neutral, global macro, and event-driven, are used by hedge funds. Every approach has a unique profile of risk and reward.

Fees: Hedge funds often impose the "2 and 20" model, which entails a management fee of 2% of assets under management and a performance fee of 20% of earnings.

Impact: Hedge funds have a big influence on market pricing and liquidity because of their scale and aggressive methods.

Partnership Funds

Mutual funds buy a diverse portfolio of stocks, bonds, and other assets by pooling the capital of many participants. They provide individual investors access to diverse portfolios without needing sizable funds and are managed by qualified portfolio managers.

Types: Mutual funds are available in equities, bonds, indexes, and balanced fund varieties. The risk and return characteristics of each category vary.

Advantages: Mutual funds are favored by regular investors because they provide liquidity, expert management, and diversity.

Fees: Management fees are paid by investors to defray the cost of running the fund. When shares are purchased or sold, certain mutual funds further impose sales loads, or fees.

Reserves for Pensions

Pension funds oversee employees' and retirees' retirement assets. Contributions are gathered and invested in order to benefit members in the future. Typically, pension funds are big, long-term investors that want steady, low-risk returns.

Types: While defined contribution plans, such as 401(k)s, rely on contributions and investment performance, defined benefit plans guarantee a predetermined monthly payout at retirement.

Investment Strategies: To balance risk and return, pension funds often make a variety of investments in stocks, bonds, real estate, and other assets.

Regulation: To make sure pension funds can fulfill their long-term responsibilities to beneficiaries, they are subject to stringent regulatory scrutiny.

Institutional investors are vital to the financial markets because they provide money, stability, and liquidity in the form of hedge funds, mutual funds, and pension funds.

Retail Investors

Individual Traders and Investors

Unlike institutional investors who oversee huge sums of money, retail investors are individual investors who purchase and sell assets for their own accounts. Retail investors may be anything from aggressive day traders to long-term buy-and-hold investors.

Single Investors

Typically, individual investors use exchange-traded funds (ETFs), mutual funds, equities, and bonds to attain their financial objectives, which may include building wealth, paying education, or saving for retirement.

Investment Strategies: These consist of income, growth, value, and buy-and-hold strategies. Every approach fits a range of risk tolerances and financial objectives.

Difficulties: Information scarcity, emotive judgment, and a lack of diversification are common difficulties faced by individual investors.

Resources: Online brokerage services, financial advisers, and robo-advisors—which provide automated investment advice—are among the tools and resources accessible to individual investors.

Traders by Day

Retail investors that aggressively purchase and sell assets within a single trading day in an attempt to benefit from transient market swings are known as day traders. It takes a lot of experience, knowledge, and a high risk tolerance to day trade.

Techniques: Typical strategies include technical analysis (using charts and indicators to anticipate price changes), momentum trading (capitalizing on surging stocks), and scalping (making several little transactions for minor returns).

Risks: Day trading has a high risk of significant losses due to its highly speculative nature. Technical analysis, risk management, and market mechanics must all be well understood.

Regulations: Day traders in the United States are governed by the Pattern Day Trader (PDT) regulation, which mandates that they execute four or more day trades in a five-day period and maintain a minimum balance of $25,000 in a margin account.

Retail investors are essential to the financial markets because they provide liquidity and influence market dynamics. They may be either long-term or active-day traders. Their involvement demonstrates a range of approaches and tolerance for risk.

Policies and Regulators

Financial, CFTC, and SEC Regulations

The integrity, openness, and stability of the financial markets depend on regulators and regulations. Important regulatory agencies that regulate various facets of the financial markets include the Commodity Futures Trading Commission (CFTC) and the Securities and Exchange Commission (SEC).

The SEC, or Securities and Exchange Commission,

The SEC is in charge of safeguarding investors, preserving fair and efficient markets, and promoting capital creation as the principal regulator of the securities industry in the United States.

Functions: The SEC manages securities exchanges, supervises brokerage houses, mutual funds, and investment counselors. It also enforces securities laws. To maintain openness, financial information must be disclosed by publicly traded corporations.

Key laws: The Securities Act of 1933, which controls the issuing of securities, and the Securities Exchange Act of 1934, which controls secondary trading, are two of the most important laws.

Enforcement: To safeguard investors and maintain market integrity, the SEC looks into and prosecutes cases of insider trading, securities fraud, and other infractions.

The CFTC, or Commodity Futures Trading Commission,

The U.S. derivatives markets, which include futures, options, and swaps, are governed by the CFTC, which also makes sure that these markets function fairly and openly.

Functions: The Consumer Financial Protection Commission (CFTC) regulates exchanges and clearinghouses, upholds laws against fraud and market manipulation, and defends investors.

Key Regulations: The Commodity Exchange Act (CEA), which aims to foster market efficiency and competition, serves as the cornerstone for CFTC monitoring.

Market Surveillance: To identify and stop abusive behaviors like manipulation and disruptive trading, the CFTC keeps an eye on trade activity.

Credit Guidelines

A wide set of guidelines and norms known as financial regulations are put in place to safeguard investors, encourage market stability, and lower systemic risk.

The Dodd-Frank Act: The Dodd-Frank Wall Street Reform and Consumer Protection Act, which was passed in reaction to the 2008 financial crisis, brought about a number of important regulatory improvements that improved risk management, increased transparency, and safeguarded consumers. Important clauses include the Volcker Rule, which limits banks' ability to trade proprietary securities, and the establishment of the Consumer Financial Protection Bureau (CFPB).

Basel III: An international regulatory framework designed to improve bank supervision, regulation, and risk control. In order to improve financial stability, it sets stricter liquidity restrictions and capital requirements.

The Sarbanes-Oxley Act: Developed in reaction to corporate scandals, this law strengthened financial transparency and corporate governance by imposing more stringent accounting and disclosure standards on publicly traded corporations.

Regulations' Impact

In order to safeguard investors and preserve market trust, regulations are essential. They assist in reducing systemic risks, ensuring fair business procedures, and preventing fraud. Regulatory systems must, however, strike a balance between promoting innovation and market expansion and control.

We have looked at the major participants in the financial markets, including institutional and individual investors, as well as the regulatory organizations that monitor and influence market behavior in this section of *The Real Deal: How Money and Markets Actually Work*. A thorough understanding of the financial landscape is possible through an understanding of the functions and interconnections of various institutions, underscoring the significance of laws in maintaining the integrity and stability of the market.

CHAPTER 5

WORLDWIDE VIEWS

International Trade

International Trade and Markets

The exchange of products, services, and money across international boundaries is known as international commerce. It enables nations to focus on producing products and services in areas where they have a competitive advantage, which boosts productivity and spurs economic expansion.

International Marketplaces

Global markets are networks of linked places where products and services are exchanged across borders. Through these marketplaces, nations may get a greater range of goods and services than they could create on their own. Important elements of worldwide marketplaces consist of:

Exporters and Importers: nations that purchase products and services from other nations and those who sell them (export).

Trade Agreements: These are bilateral and multilateral agreements that lower tariffs, quotas, and other trade restrictions between nations. The European Union (EU) and the North American Free Trade Agreement (NAFTA) are two examples.

Global Supply Chains: intricate international manufacturing and distribution networks. A smartphone, for example, may be manufactured in China, built in different regions of Asia, and designed in the United States.

Commerce Regulations

A nation's laws and policies governing international commerce are known as its trade policy. The following policies have the potential to have a major effect on the world economy:

Tariffs: Import taxes that raise the cost of commodities and reduce their ability to compete with native ones. Tariffs are meant to shield home industries, but if they are retaliated upon, they may start trade wars.

Quotas: Restrictions on the amount of a product that may be imported, which shield home manufacturers from outside rivalry.

Subsidies: Governments provide local businesses with financial support to increase the competitiveness of their goods on the international market.

Trade obstacles: non-tariff trade obstacles that have the potential to impede free commerce include licensing requirements, import restrictions, and regulatory standards.

Effect of Trade Regulations

Trade agreements may have a significant impact on economies.

Economic Growth: By broadening markets and promoting innovation, free trade policies may boost economic growth.

Employment: While trade may boost employment in export-oriented sectors, it can also result in job losses in areas where international competition is present.

Consumer costs: By making cheaper imported items more widely available, free trade may reduce consumer costs.

Understanding international commerce and trade policy is essential to understanding the global economic environment and the economic interactions between nations.

Emerging Markets

Possibilities and Hazards

Economies in emerging markets are those that are rapidly industrializing and growing. These markets have a lot to offer investors, but there are a lot of hazards as well.

Chances in Developing Markets

Emerging markets provide a range of prospects.

High Growth Potential: When compared to industrialized economies, emerging countries often see greater rates of economic growth. Industrialization and urbanization have fueled significant growth rates in nations like China, India, and Brazil.

Varieties of Investment Options: Stocks, bonds, and real estate are just a few of the many investment options available in these markets.

Demographic Trends: A greater workforce and more consumer demand are the results of the youthful, expanding populations in many developing economies.

Dangers in Developing Economies

Investing in developing economies has a number of risks.

Political Instability: Uncertainty in politics and problems with governance may cause abrupt changes in economic policies that have an effect on investments.

Currency Risk: The value of assets denominated in foreign currencies may fluctuate due to fluctuations in exchange rates.

Market Volatility: Because of their less developed financial systems and lower market liquidity, emerging markets may be more erratic.

Regulatory Risks: Laws and regulations may change suddenly in developing economies, creating uncertain regulatory environments.

Investing Techniques for Developing Markets

Investors may use a variety of techniques to manage the potential and dangers in developing markets, including:

Diversification: To reduce risk, distribute investments throughout a number of nations and industries.

Due Diligence: Investigating and analyzing in-depth to comprehend particular dangers and possibilities in every industry.

Long-term Perspective: Paying more attention

to prospects for long-term growth than to gyrations in the market.

The investing environment in emerging nations is dynamic and potentially lucrative, but it also demands cautious thought and risk management.

Economic Indicators

GDP, Employment Rates, and Inflation

Economic indicators are numbers that show how well and in which direction an economy is doing. The GDP, inflation, and employment rates are some of the most significant statistics.

GDP, or gross domestic product

The total worth of all products and services produced in a nation during a certain time period is its GDP. It is a crucial sign of development and activity in the economy.

Components: Government expenditure, investment, consumption, and net exports (exports less imports) make up GDP.

Types of GDP: Real GDP accounts for inflation and provides a more realistic picture of economic growth than nominal GDP, which values goods and services at current prices.

Importance: GDP growth rates show how well an economy is doing. A recession may be indicated by negative growth, while positive growth points to an increase in the economy.

Inflation

The pace at which prices for goods and services are generally increasing and decreasing buying power is known as inflation.

Causes: Rising production costs, monetary factors (increasing money supply), and demand-pull forces (increased demand for products and services) may all lead to inflation.

Measurement: Two widely used indicators of inflation are the Producer Price Index (PPI) and the Consumer Price Index (CPI). While the PPI examines variations in wholesale prices, the CPI follows changes in the prices of a basket of consumer goods and services.

Impact: While deflation (negative inflation) may result in a decline in economic activity, excessive inflation can lower buying power and savings. Moderate inflation is a sign of a thriving economy.

Rates of Employment

Economic stability and the labor market are both reflected in employment rates.

Unemployment Rate: The proportion of jobless individuals actively looking for jobs. A strong labor market is shown by low unemployment, but high unemployment is a sign of an economic crisis.

Labor Force Participation Rate: The proportion of individuals of working age who are either employed or actively looking for a job. This rate aids in understanding labor availability.

Types of Unemployment: seasonal (variations in labor demand throughout the year), cyclical (caused by economic downturns), structural (mismatch between skills and jobs), and frictional (short-term, transitional).

Economic Indicators Interpreted

Businesses, investors, and regulators utilize economic indicators to help them make choices.

Policymakers: Manage economic growth and stability by creating and implementing monetary and fiscal policies based on indications.

Investors: Use indicator analysis to predict economic trends, evaluate market conditions, and decide what to buy.

Businesses: Make use of indicators to manage resources, plan for growth, and modify pricing strategies.

This last section of "The Real Deal: How Money and Markets Actually Work, delves into the economics of the world. A thorough understanding of the global economy may be obtained by familiarizing oneself with major economic indicators, emerging market opportunities and risks, and international commerce. With this information, you can successfully navigate the increasingly international financial world.

CHAPTER 6

REAL-WORLD APPLICATIONS

Personal Finance

Saving, Investing, and Budgeting

The foundation of financial well-being is personal finance, which includes the choices and tactics people use to successfully manage their finances. Investing, saving, and budgeting are important components.

Planning

The act of making a plan for your financial expenditures is known as budgeting. You can limit your spending, manage your income, and reach your financial objectives with the aid of this financial road map.

Money and Expenses: To begin, list all of your monthly outlays, including variables (such as food and entertainment) and fixed (such as rent and utilities).

Setting Priorities: Before spending money on desires, divide your income among your basic necessities, such as shelter, food, and transportation.

Savings Objectives: List savings as an absolute must. Set aside a certain portion of your monthly income for emergencies, retirement, and other financial objectives.

Reserving

Savings are essential for reaching long-term objectives and ensuring financial stability. It offers a basis for future investments as well as a safety net for emergencies.

Emergency Reserve: Set aside three to six months' worth of living costs to create an emergency reserve. You will be shielded against monetary shocks such as job loss or unexpected medical expenses by this fund.

Short-term Goals: Set aside money for upcoming trips, a new vehicle, or a down payment on a home. For superior interest rates and ease of access, choose high-yield savings accounts.

Automate Savings: To guarantee regular savings, set up automatic transfers from your checking account to your savings account.

Investing

Investing is the act of employing capital to purchase assets with the hope of making a profit or revenue. It is necessary to gradually accumulate riches.

Investment possibilities: real estate, equities, bonds, and mutual funds are examples of common investment possibilities. Each has unique features related to risk and reward.

Diversification: To lower risk, distribute your assets across a variety of asset types. Having a diverse portfolio helps shield it from market fluctuations.

Long-term Perspective: Pay more attention to sustained growth than to cyclical changes in the market. To ensure that your investing plan is in line with your objectives, examine and tweak it often.

Budgeting, saving, and investing are all important components of effective personal finance management, which enables people to attain financial stability and gradually accumulate wealth.

Financial Management

How Businesses Obtain and Handle Funds

Corporate finance is the study of how businesses generate, manage, and distribute money in order to maximize value. It encompasses all financial aspects of operating a firm.

Capital Raising

Businesses raise money to invest in new ventures, grow, and finance operations. Debt finance and equity financing are the two main approaches.

Equity Financing: This method entails obtaining money by offering investors shares of the business. Common forms consist of the issuance of preferred and common stock.

Benefits: No interest payments; no need to reimburse investors.

Disadvantages: Diluting ownership; stockholders may be entitled to dividends.

Debt Financing: This refers to taking out loans, bonds, or credit lines to borrow money.

Benefits: Interest payments are tax deductible; you keep full ownership.

Disadvantages: interest-bearing need; elevated risk to finances during recessions.

Capital Management

The long-term performance and financial stability of a corporation are dependent on effective capital management.

Working Capital Management: Making sure the business has enough liquid assets to pay for liquid debt. Keeping track of inventories, accounts payable, and receivable is essential.

Capital Budgeting: Assessing and choosing long-term investment initiatives according to their likelihood of producing a return. The payback period, internal rate of return (IRR), and net present value (NPV) are examples of these techniques.

Capital Structure: Choosing the Best Ratio of Debt to Equity Funding The objective is to maximize shareholder value while minimizing the cost of capital.

Planning and Analysis of Finances

Making well-informed judgments requires regular strategic planning and financial analysis.

Financial Statements: Examining the cash flow, income, and balance sheets to gauge the health and performance of the company's finances.

Projecting future income, costs, and cash flows to inform strategic planning and decision-making is known as "forecasting.

Risk Management: Using techniques for insurance, diversification, and hedging, one may identify and reduce financial risks.

Gaining knowledge of corporate finance facilitates understanding of how businesses raise, handle, and distribute resources to achieve sustainability and growth.

Financial Disasters

Origins, Effects, and Recuperation

Economic crises are characterized by significant interruptions to the economy, as seen by drops in GDP, elevated jobless rates, and unstable financial markets. To navigate and mitigate their effects, it is essential to comprehend their sources, consequences, and recovery procedures.

Reasons for Financial Crisis

Numerous, often intricately linked elements might set off an economic crisis.

Financial bubbles: quick rises in asset values that are followed by steep drops. One example is the housing bubble, which sparked the financial crisis of 2008.

Banking Failures: As shown by the Great Depression and the 2008 financial crisis, insolvency or illiquidity in the banking sector may cause a credit crunch.

Sovereign Debt Crises: These occur when nations can't pay back their debt, which triggers defaults and unstable economies. One such example is the debt crisis in Europe.

External Shocks: Unexpected outside events that might affect economies include changes in the price of oil, natural catastrophes, or geopolitical unrest.

Policy Failures: Economic downturns may be made worse by foolish fiscal or monetary policies. For example, during a recession, strict monetary policy may exacerbate the decline in the economy.

Economic Crisis Impacts

Economic crises affect economies and society broadly and severely.

jobless: As companies eliminated staff to save money, jobless rates rose sharply.

GDP Decline: Notable declines in economic growth and production.

Financial Instability: Market volatility that lowers consumer confidence and investment.

Social Consequences: As vulnerable groups are impacted by economic woes, there will be a rise in poverty, inequality, and social unrest.

Recovery from Financial Disasters

Coordinated efforts by governments, central banks, and international organizations are necessary to recover from an economic crisis.

Monetary Policy: To encourage borrowing, spending, and investment, central banks often lower interest rates and carry out quantitative easing.

Fiscal Policy: To stimulate the economy and assist impacted people and companies, governments may lower taxes and increase public expenditure.

Structural changes: putting policies in place to strengthen economic resilience, such as investment in infrastructure, labor market changes, and financial regulation.

International Cooperation: coordinated actions taken by global institutions such as the World Bank and the International Monetary Fund (IMF) to provide impacted nations with financial assistance and policy recommendations.

Studies of Cases

The Great Depression: Started by the 1929 stock market collapse, it resulted in deflation and massive unemployment. World War II expenditures and New Deal initiatives were part of the recovery.

The 2008 Financial Crisis: This recession was brought on by financial institutions and the property market collapsing. Bailouts, regulatory changes, and significant monetary stimulus were all part of the recovery.

Individuals, companies, and politicians may

better plan for and react to future economic shocks by having a better understanding of the origins, effects, and recovery processes of economic crises.

This last section of "The Real Deal: How Money and Markets Actually Work, has covered the real-world applications of financial concepts in the areas of corporate finance, personal finance, and crisis management. The significance of financial literacy in maneuvering through the intricacies of the contemporary economy and attaining economic prosperity and steadiness is underscored by these pragmatic implementations.

CHAPTER 7

THE FUTURE OF MONEY AND MARKETS

Innovation and Fintech

Blockchain Technology and Digital Currency

The boom in financial technology, or fintech, is changing how we engage with money and markets. Digital currencies and blockchain technology, which have the potential to completely change financial institutions and transactions, are essential to this shift.

Electronic Money

Money is being redefined by digital currencies, such as cryptocurrencies and central bank digital currencies (CBDCs).

Cryptocurrencies: Blockchain technology is used by Bitcoin, Ethereum, and other cryptocurrencies to run on decentralized networks. They provide an alternative to conventional financial institutions in the form of a new kind of digital asset.

Bitcoin: The first and best-known cryptocurrency, often called "digital gold" because of its ability to hold value.

Ethereum: Well-known for its smart contract features, which let programmers create decentralized apps (dApps) on its network.

Benefits: Reduced transaction costs, quicker international transfers, and enhanced security and privacy are all provided by cryptocurrencies.

Difficulties: There are still a number of important difficulties, including price volatility, regulatory uncertainty, and security issues (such as hacking).

Central Bank Digital Currencies (CBDCs): In an effort to update financial systems, governments and central banks are investigating CBDCs.

Purpose: The goal of CBDCs is to provide a digital currency that is stable, guaranteed by the government, and can improve payment systems and financial inclusion.

Examples: Two of the most prominent CBDC projects are Sweden's e-Krona and China's Digital Yuan.

Implications: CBDCs may lessen the need for hard currency, expedite the application of monetary policy, and provide more effective ways to make payments.

Crypto Blockchain

The underlying technology of cryptocurrencies, the blockchain, provides a decentralized, transparent, and safe ledger system.

How It Works: Transactions are recorded in blocks on a blockchain, which are connected by links. To guarantee data integrity and security, every block includes a timestamp and a cryptographic hash of the block before it.

Uses Not Limited to Cryptocurrency:

Smart Contracts: Automated and trustless transactions made possible by self-executing contracts with terms encoded straight into code.

Supply Chain Management: By providing a tamper-proof record of product movement, supply networks may be made more transparent and traceable.

Identification Verification: Providing safe, decentralized methods for confirming an individual's identification in order to guard against fraud.

The Fintech Future

Fintech advancements have the potential to further upend established financial services while encouraging increased productivity, diversity, and creativity. Digital currencies and blockchain technology are going to become more and more important components of the global financial system.

Sustainable Investing

Ethical Investing and ESG Criteria

A rising understanding of how investments affect society and the environment is reflected in sustainable investing, which incorporates environmental, social, and governance (ESG) factors into investment choices.

Requirements for ESG

A framework for assessing the ethical and sustainable effects of investments is provided by ESG criteria.

Environmental: Concentrates on how an organization utilizes resources, manages waste, uses energy efficiently, and has an influence on the environment.

Social: evaluates how a business interacts with its community, suppliers, consumers, and workers. Human rights, labor practices, and community involvement are important variables.

Governance: Assesses the caliber of a business's executive pay, diversity on the board, and financial reporting transparency.

ESG Investing Benefits

Investing in ESG has several benefits.

Risk Management: Businesses that have robust ESG policies are often better run and face less risks to their reputation, the environment, and the law.

Long-term Performance: Because they are better equipped to handle obstacles and seize opportunities down the road, sustainable businesses often outperform others in the long run.

Good Impact: ESG investing links financial decisions with individual values by promoting businesses that have a good social and environmental impact.

Investing Ethically

Ethical investing takes into account the moral and ethical ramifications of investment decisions in addition to financial gains.

Socially Responsible Investing (SRI): Steers clear of businesses that are seen to be detrimental, such as fossil fuels, tobacco, and weaponry.

effect investing: concentrates on producing quantifiable financial rewards in addition to social and environmental effects. Investments in affordable housing, education, and renewable energy are a few examples.

Faith-based investing avoids industries or activities that go against religious principles and ideals in order to align investments with such values.

Sustainable Investment's Future

Growing public knowledge of global issues such as social injustice and climate change is leading to a mainstreaming of sustainable investment. Investors are becoming more aware of how including ESG criteria may improve risk-adjusted returns and help create a more fair and sustainable society.

Forecasting Trends in the Market

Instruments and Methods

One of the most difficult yet important parts of effective investment is predicting market movements. Investors may predict market fluctuations and make well-informed choices by using a variety of tools and approaches.

Technical Evaluation

Technical analysis is the process of forecasting future market behavior by examining past price and volume data.

Charts and Patterns: Instruments that assist in determining possible market directions include trend lines, candlestick charts, and chart patterns (such as head and shoulders and double tops).

Indicators and Oscillators: Measures that reveal market momentum, volatility, and possible turning points include moving averages, the Relative Strength Index (RSI), and Bollinger Bands.

Elementary Examination

A company's intrinsic worth is evaluated by fundamental analysis using financial statements, market circumstances, and economic variables.

Financial Ratios: Ratios that provide light on a company's value and financial health include price-to-earnings (P/E), debt-to-equity (D/E), and return on equity (ROE).

Economic Indicators: Interest rates, GDP growth, inflation rates, and unemployment statistics all affect the state of the market and investor mood.

Industry Analysis: Recognizing possibilities and hazards for development within an industry is facilitated by an understanding of its competitive landscape, market trends, and regulatory framework.

Methodological Evaluation

Quantitative analysis looks for trends in the market and potential investments using statistical methods and mathematical models.

Algorithms and AI: To identify patterns, enhance trading tactics, and control risk, sophisticated algorithms and artificial intelligence (AI) evaluate huge datasets.

Backtesting: Testing trading methods using past data to assess their efficacy and make necessary adjustments before implementing them in live markets.

Emotional Dissection

In order to forecast market trends, sentiment research measures investors' and market participants' emotions.

News and Social Media: To get insight into investor emotions and possible market responses, one might analyze news headlines, social media postings, and market comments.

Surveys and Indices: Instruments that shed light on investor expectations and the state of the market include the Consumer Confidence Index (CCI) and the American Association of Individual Investors (AAII) mood survey.

Market Predictions Future

It is probable that technological developments such as artificial intelligence (AI), machine learning, and big data analytics will propel market prediction in the future. With the help of these technologies, it will be easier to analyze large volumes of data and spot minute patterns, which will increase the precision and potency of market forecasts.

The future of money and markets has been examined in this last section of *The Real Deal: How Money and Markets Actually Work. We've looked at how fintech breakthroughs, sustainable investment, and cutting-edge prediction technologies are influencing the financial landscape. These trends draw attention to how dynamic and ever-changing the financial industry is, highlighting the need for flexibility and never-ending education to survive and prosper in this always-shifting landscape.

CONCLUSION

We congratulate you on finishing "The Real Deal: How Money and Markets Really Work"! You have been taken on an insightful journey through the complex realms of finance and economics throughout this book, covering foundational ideas, new developments, and real-world applications. As you contemplate your educational experience, bear in mind the following important lessons:

Integrating Information

Putting Your Knowledge to Use

You now have a thorough knowledge of a wide range of financial and economic concepts thanks to your experience with "The Real Deal. It's now time to apply that understanding:

Personal Finance: Use investment, saving, and budgeting techniques to reach your financial objectives and safeguard your future. Make sure your spending and income are in balance, save aside money for long-term objectives and emergencies first, and make prudent investments to increase your wealth over time.

Corporate Finance: Gain insight into how businesses raise and handle cash to evaluate company prospects and make well-informed investment choices. Examine financial documents, assess the profitability and performance of the firm, and, using strong financial analysis, identify investment prospects.

Economic Analysis: Forecast changes in the economy and formulate strategic judgments by using market trends and economic data. Keep yourself updated on world events, governmental initiatives, and macroeconomic trends that might affect financial markets and investment prospects.

Risk Management: Use insurance, diversification, and wise investing techniques to identify and reduce financial risks. Create a well-balanced investment portfolio that fits your risk appetite and financial objectives by being aware of the dangers connected to various asset classes and evaluating your risk tolerance.

Ethical Investing: Use sustainable investing to make investments that will have a beneficial social and environmental effect and match your financial decisions with your values. When assessing investment prospects, take environmental, social, and governance (ESG) factors into account. Additionally, provide assistance to businesses that exhibit sustainability efforts and ethical business practices.

You may make better financial choices and confidently and clearly navigate the intricacies of today's financial world by using the information you've received from *The Real Deal.

Keeping Up-to-Date

Materials and Ongoing Instruction

Success in the dynamic fields of finance and economics depends on knowledge retention. To help you on your learning path, consider the following tools and techniques:

Books and Publications: Learn about a variety of publications, periodicals, and books on finance, economics, and related subjects. Seek reliable resources that provide in-depth analysis and insights on the most recent advancements and trends in the financial sector.

Online Courses and Webinars: Participate in webinars and online courses that colleges, financial institutions, and trade associations are offering. These platforms provide quick and easy methods to increase your understanding and proficiency in certain financial and economics-related fields.

Financial News and Analysis: Keep up with the most recent information on the financial industry from reliable publications like The Wall Street Journal, Bloomberg, and Financial Times. For knowledgeable views and analysis on market trends and economic events, follow reputable economists, analysts, and pundits.

Professional organizations: To network with colleagues in the field, get resources, and remain up-to-date on trends and advancements in the sector, become a member of professional organizations and economics and finance networking groups. To meet new people and share ideas with colleagues, go to conferences, seminars, and networking events.

Continuing Education: To strengthen your qualifications and level of competence in certain areas of finance and economics, pursue certificates, designations, and continuing education courses. Depending on your interests and professional ambitions, take into consideration programs like the Certified Financial Planner (CFP) certification, the Certified Economic Developer (CEcD) designation, or the Chartered Financial Analyst (CFA) designation.

Networking and Mentoring: Establish connections with mentors, associates, and business experts who may provide direction, encouragement, and development prospects. Take advantage of networking events and mentoring opportunities to learn from and get viewpoints from seasoned industry experts.

In the fast-paced world of finance and economics, you may accomplish your professional and financial objectives by keeping up with the latest developments and never stopping learning.

Concluding Remarks

As you get to the end of your reading of "The Real Deal: How Money and Markets Actually Work, keep in mind that economics and finance are dynamic, multidimensional subjects. Accept curiosity, lifelong learning, and critical thinking as you make your way through the intricacies of markets and money. The information and insights you've learned from *The Real Deal* will enable you to make wise choices, generate value, and contribute to a more affluent and sustainable future—whether you're an investor, entrepreneur, policymaker, or just a curious learner. We appreciate you coming along on this insightful trip with us, and we wish you success, happiness, and continuous progress in all of your financial endeavors.

www.ingramcontent.com/pod-product-compliance
Lightning Source LLC
Chambersburg PA
CBHW050108230526
45470CB00004B/1737